Michael Paraskos

Four Essays on
Art and Anarchism

The **Orage** Press
2015

Published by the Orage Press.

The Orage Press
16A Heaton Road
Mitcham
Surrey
CR4 2BU
England

ISBN: 978-0-9929247-9-9

Printed by Lightningsource

Michael Paraskos

Four Essays on
Art and Anarchism

Contents

Michael Paraskos is a lecturer at the
City and Guilds of London Art School

Introduction

The relationship between art and anarchism has a long but often hidden history. Artists as diverse as Courbet, Pissarro, Seurat, Signac, van Gogh, Kandinsky, Tatlin, Gris, and many others, have been positively identified as being anarchists, or as having sympathies with anarchist ideas, but for me there is an argument to be made that anarchist ideas are at the heart of all acts of artistic creation.

I suspect I pursue a version of this belief in almost everything I write on art and other topics, and so I am a little wary of publishing these essays in a form that might be seen by some people as an evangelical sermon. Most of the essays that form the chapters of this little book began life as independent lectures, delivered at different times and at various venues around the world. Consequently they were never intended to act either as definitions of anarchist art, or as a manifesto for future activity by anyone who wants to call themselves an anarchist artist. Rather they are statements on various aspects of the relationship between art and anarchism that

I see, and which I believe are essential to both. *As they were, so they remain,* neither a sermon nor a manifesto, but a series of personal observations based on personal experiences. There will be other statements, by other people, perhaps carrying much more weight than mine, but these are my opinions, take them or leave them.

In saying that (and another cause of my wariness) I should explain that I do not label myself as an anarchist and have never done so. The term syndicalist would probably fit me better, if I was forced to choose, but even in that I much prefer the now rather unfashionable term, *co-operator.* No doubt this is partly due to a sentimental and nostalgic affection I carry in me for the long-since defunct Leeds Industrial Co-operative Society, in the café of which I spent many lunchtimes eating cheap meals as a student. But it all means my right to speak on behalf of anyone calling themselves an anarchist is nonexistent, and quite rightly so. That said, anarchism is still to my mind the most useful tool for both makers and viewers of art to help us identify, understand and assert the function of art in society.

As will be clear from this small selection of essays I come to the question of art and anarchism from a particular perspective which links all four essays. Of course there will be other definitions of anarchist art that are just as valid, particularly in relation to the place of art in direct action and its role in highlighting social ills, and in no sense am I dismissing those definitions. I suppose the issue has really to be reversed to say that, just as I am happy to accept other definitions of anarchist art, so I would hope the adherents to those definitions would reciprocate, and accept that my perspective has a right to be aired also.

That perspective is one I like, somewhat quixotically, to call exotic anarchism, not as a banner under which I plan to march, but as a simple description. It is exotic insofar as I view the role of art in human society and the individual human psyche as a means to step outside of the known world into the *exoticness* of other worlds, not as a pseudo-mystical exercise, but as a necessary social, intellectual and emotional process. I am tempted to liken this view of art to the sandbox function on Wikipedia, which allows members of the Wikipedia community to test ideas and develop new ways of thinking. To maintain this analogy we would have to agree that although the Wiki sandbox does exist it is in a sense outside the 'real' world of Wikipedia. It is not an elegant analogy, but it is not far from what I am proposing.

Following on from this, even if we reject the *potentially* mystical notion of art existing outside everyday reality, I believe it is still useful to conceptualise art *as if* it allows us to step outside reality. By doing so we give ourselves a space in which to imagine other ways of being, a space in which it is possible to imagine life in all its forms, existing in radically different ways to how it exists now. In a sense I could call it a space in which to dream, but I fear that will sound somewhat fey. Perhaps one might say instead, it is a space in which to desire, fear and propose, but in each attempt to define the nature of this space we keep coming up against its ineluctable mystery, its essential otherness to what we know now, that makes it function in the first place.

As Herbert Read suggested, there has to be a vital link between art and life to stop art descending into decadent fantasy, but at the same time, if we also fall into the trap that art is no more than a mirror held up to life then we might as well stick with life itself. If we did that, we might justly say we are all material realists, but we would also risk losing a potent tool for imagining radically different worlds in which things are done radically differently. We would risk losing the imagination as a tool for revolutionary change.

In all of this I am guided by a longstanding admiration for the writings of Herbert Read, whose presence haunted many of the original talks I gave and continues into these essays. But I am also enamoured by writers on art as diverse as Charles Fourier, Max Blechman, John Farquhar McLay and Cindy Milstein, amongst others, whose spirit, and sometimes direct words, also find their way into these essays.

For the record, *To Hell with Culture: To Heaven with Art* began life, under the title *What would an anarchist Rembrandt look like?*, delivered as a talk at the University of Loughborough in 2012. *The Table Top Schools of Art* began as a lecture at the Cyprus College of Art I think in 2005 (or thereabouts). *An Anarchist in Heaven and Hell* was originally a talk given at the International Anthony Burgess Foundation in Manchester in 2014. And *The Canvas as*

Commune began as an exhibition catalogue, for a show entitled *The Anarchists*, held in Nicosia, Cyprus in 2007. However, various versions of these talks have also been aired elsewhere, and they are part of an ongoing process.

To Hell with Culture:
To Heaven with Art

The sculptor Eric Gill is not much considered in anarchist circles these days, but in his lifetime he was acknowledged as a significant figure for his discussion of art and culture from an anarchist perspective. Gill wrote:

> When will the revolutionary leaders realise that culture is dope, a worse dope than religion; for even if it were true that religion is the opiate of the people, it is worse to poison yourself than to be poisoned, and suicide is more dishonourable than murder. To hell with culture, culture as a thing added like a sauce to otherwise unpalatable stale fish! [1]

To hell with culture says Gill. That phrase became the title of an essay by Herbert Read in 1943, and in turn became the title of Read's 1963 book. And in direct homage to Read in 2005 it also became the title for a book by H. Gustav Klaus and Stephen Knight on the impact of anarchism on twentieth-century British literature.

But what did Gill and Read mean by to hell with culture? An answer might lie in an interview with Read conducted by the anarchist painter Victor Willing in 1960.[2]

There Read suggested the best thing to do with the art schools would be to close them down as they simply taught cliches of art, not art itself.[3] That is to say the art schools taught culture and not art.

In this we have a Readian sense that art is distinct from culture and in that distinction we find a clue to the desire by the likes of Gill and Read to dispense with culture. To hell with culture because for people like Read culture is an imposed theory of society. To hell with culture because far more fundamentally than the government, or the economically dominant class, or the other institutional agents of social control, culture is the state. To hell with culture because culture stands between the individual and him or herself.

Making a distinction between art and culture might be difficult for cultural theorists and historians today to accept. The thrust of academic debate for the past half century has been to deny any difference between the two and because of this we have inherited a way of thinking about art that says it is a part of culture. This is the mainstream academic view of art and culture, but it is a view that is also dominant well beyond the mainstream, so that many present-day anarchists too would readily accept that art is a part of culture.

But what if we attempt something different, so that in the context of what we might call anarchist cultural studies, or anarchist art history, or simply anarchism, we question a mainstream view like this?

As a general principle, I think, a good starting point for any dissenting political and cultural movement is to dissent, by which I mean it is a good idea to question and doubt the accepted wisdom of mainstream views. That is not to say we should act as nihilists at each and every juncture, but it seems logical to assume that in a society which is based on precepts that are predominantly opposed to those of anarchism, the cynicism of Diogenes is a healthy starting point for any anarchist to hold. And on that basis, when casting an eye over the study of art, we might not want to take for granted the validity of any mainstream view even when it is dressed up as radical.

For example, we might not automatically accept the radicalism of the views of John Molyneux when he writes:

> In my opinion the starting point for understanding both the nature of Dutch society in the Golden Age... and the nature of Rembrandt's art... is that the Dutch Republic was the world's first properly capitalist society and state, the result of the first successful bourgeois revolution.[4]

Here Molyneux writes from the perspective of a marxist, but the views he expresses are also the mainstream views for most academic art theorists and historians, marxist or not. They are derived from an understanding of art that says we should view it either wholly or predominantly as a reflection of the social structures of society, primarily the class structures.

Unsurprisingly this view of art had its origins in the marxist phenomenon of the New Art History that came to dominate the understanding of art in universities, particularly in Britain and North America, from the 1970s onwards. As the Glaswegian anarchist activist John Farquhar McLay noted back in 1982, it is predicated on the fact that, 'For marxists art has no primary dynamic. It is to be accounted for in the usual way through an economic analysis of society.' In that, he says, art is not seen as embodying the human spirit, imagination or 'the most personal part of man.' Instead 'The marxist simply sees art as a class tool expressing class interests.'[5] In other words for the marxist art is a part of bourgeois culture.

I am not proposing to offer a critique of the restricted approach of art embodied in the New Art History. I simply note that despite his radical credentials, Molyneux's view of art is very much the mainstream academic view. And in that I offer a cautionary word from the perspective of Diogenes. The New Art History embedded in the universities a marxist derived methodology for understanding art with such success it is difficult now not only to find, but to imagine, any form of art history, marxist or otherwise, that does not derive its ultimate methodology from the New Art History.

But as a cynic we are surely justified in asking why a supposedly radical understanding of art based on the principle that it is an epiphenomenon, limping after reality, and reflecting the class structure of society, has found such a happy home in such a bourgeois habitat as the universities. Surely we should question how the New Art History moved so quickly from being a marxist phenomenon to what we might term a bourgeois-marxist one, with even Kate Middleton studying art history under tutors whose stated interests included 'societal tensions in Italy... and the ways in which [art] was employed by the political classes to influence public opinion and behaviour.'[6]

I have no ready answers to these questions, only the questions themselves. But they are questions that should bring even a marxist art theorist up short to ask how this could have happened? How could what was purported to be a radical understanding of art, in opposition to bourgeois values, be so fully subsumed into bourgeois life?

The answer might well lie in a fundamental unifying factor that links bourgeois ideology with marxism. In researching this paper I was shown an interesting book called *Art in Its Time*, by Paul Mattick, who is Professor of Philosophy at Adelphi University in New York. Citing Marx as an authority, Mattick suggests that under marxism: 'It is imaginable, perhaps even likely, that art would lose the special social value which today stems from its contrast with industrial production and consumption, and which enables it to function as an emblem of class superiority.' But he then adds a telling rider: 'Interestingly, something like this change in social character is already happening, as the boundaries between art and such lifestyle fields as cuisine and design, on the one hand, and commercial entertainment, on the other, are becoming increasingly permeable.'[7]

As this indicates, according to a marxist writer himself, we do not need a marxist society for a marxian ambition for art to take place. A bourgeois-capitalist one will do just as well, with Mattick seeming to suggest that the marxist project and the bourgeois capitalist project are close enough at some level to see a commensurate debasement of art. As a consequence, for an anarchist, does it not follow that such a reductivist assumption that Rembrandt's art is merely 'the result of the first successful bourgeois revolution' is at the very least problematic? Should we not entertain the possibility that Rembrandt's art might be rather more complex than this kind of glib reductivism? Such reductivism not only goes against the complex diversity of life as we experience it, but is clearly dubious in any claim it might make to be a radical analysis of art as it appears to be a view also held by some of the most deeply reactionary elements in our society. For example, you do not have to read marxist historians such as Mattick to get this kind of analysis of art, you can read a typical press release, extolling the social relevance of an artist, put out by commercial galleries such as the Saatchi. From an anarchist perspective, seeing the unholy confluence of so-called radical marxism and bourgeois capitalism in this way are we not forced to question the nature of radicalism itself?

Perhaps I can explain what I mean by means of an analogy. Imagine we are on a bus. The bus driver is taking us to where the bus company says we must go. No amount of protest or reason from the passengers will persuade the driver to deviate from the bus company's route, and if we passengers become too bolshy the driver pulls a gun on us and orders us to sit down. Occasionally he even shoots some of the passengers so we know he means it. Welcome aboard

Capital Buses. On Vanguard Buses things are different. A proletarian committee, set up by some of the more vocal passengers decides on the destination, acting in the best interests of the whole bus. Some of the passengers still disagree with the destination, but they are either locked in the boot, or shot, this time for the common good. And so we go on, like the wheels of the bus, going round and round, all day long. But as the day ends, along comes Messrs Gill and Read. They say to hell with buses. They say, stop the bus I want to get off. But how is it possible to get off the bus, asks Capital Buses, and Vanguard Buses? There is only the bus.

We seem here to be in the state of existence that filled Schopenhauer with such dread 200 years ago. He called his bus the 'Will', and to him there seemed little hope of escape from the insatiable desires of the Will except through death. The only possible hope of escape in life was the same as that proposed by Read and Gil a century later, namely art. And so, while I am not conflating Schopenhauer's conception of Will with culture, I am suggesting a typological connection between the two. We are trapped on the bus, the bus of culture or the bus of

Will. It is not through culture that one can escape this situation, but art, and that means the radicalism of Read and Gill's anarchism did not lie in taking over the bus, either collectively or individually, or even analysing the nature of the bus *ad infinitum*. It lay in getting off the bus completely, in rejecting culture completely, and in its place revealing art. If one reads Herbert Read's only finished novel, *The Green Child*, with that realisation in mind, I think that simple message is resoundingly clear.

So perhaps radicalism is not what we think it is. Perhaps too often when we think of radicalism we really cleave to a cliche of radicalism. In doing so we surely cleave to a pre-defined cultural definition of radicalism, defined by a culture we claim to despise in so many ways, rather than radicalism itself which would reject such pre-definitions.

Certainly we do not have to search far to find examples of this clichéd radicalism in our own time and their negative consequences.

In 2007 the conceptualist Mark Wallinger staged an installation at Tate Britain, called State Britain, in which he created a facsimile of the late Brian Haw's anti-war peace camp in Parliament Square.

On the surface this seemed a radical act, not least because the political narrative of Brian Haw's original peace camp was itself radical, signifying opposition to British state policy in Iraq and Afghanistan. But as Wallinger himself noted, the public perception fostered by the politically dominant classes and media was that Brian Haw was a 'crank' or 'eccentric', and so when it came to his peace camp in Parliament Square, it was only 'a limited number of people who crossed the road to look at it.'[8]

We have to recognise that Haw's initial hostility to Wallinger's installation changed over time, so that when Wallinger won the Turner Prize in 2007 Haw spoke warmly of him. From that we can deduce that Wallinger persuaded Haw that his motives were sincere. I don't think we have reason to doubt that. But what actually happened in the transfer of the peace camp from its actuality in Parliament Square to its facsimile in Tate Britain was the neutralising of the disturbing impact of the peace camp. One can see this by contrasting Parliament Square with the safe environment of Tate Britain, where the viewer might peruse the camp with its placards at his or her leisure, before heading off to have a cappuccino in the cafe or buy a postcard at the gift shop, all without the disturbing presence of Brian Haw or his fellow protestors. This is not just a matter of feeling safe from the real impact of the peace camp and its political message, it is a matter of dehumanising the camp by removing the humans from it. Most significant of all, as most of us will know, protests are unnerving because they bring you face to face with the state's security apparatuses. So Wallinger's fake peace camp neutralised the reality of protest because you could see it without fear that the authorities might view your visit as a sign of extremist political views. As Sinead Murphy has written: 'Wallinger's art work, though indiscernible from Haw's protest, was not dismantled by the police. Haw's protest, become art, had ceased to make itself heard.' In effect the transfer of Haw's peace camp to Tate Britain was a form of kettling Murphy suggests.[9]

As I say, I do not have any reason to believe this was Wallinger's intention. But as the study of semiotics has shown the understanding of narrative signifiers is not universal. Indeed social semiotics is now revealing, the lack of universality is not simply matter of whether one gets the sign or not, by which I mean reads it in the way intended or not. Rather it is, as Carey Jewitt and Rumiko Oyama have described, a question of who controls the context in which the signifier or narrative is placed.[10]

Tate Britain is a state institution and so it would be naive to believe that it could ever act against the interests of the state. But more disturbing is the subtle neutralising of radicalism it achieves, possibly in spite of the aims of any protagonists.

This might suggest the placing of art in a non-radical space like the Tate turns it into culture, and so the answer is to reject such institutions for art, to keep art active in society. Certainly many anarchists have advocated this, even arguing, like Kropotkin, that in an anarchist society there would be no artists because everything each human being would do would be done in the spirit of art. A separate category of art made by artists would be redundant.[11]

In our society this attitude is most often seen in the diverse phenomena of street art that is often associated with anarchism. But even here we should cast the eye of Diogenes the Cynic over what actually occurs, and question whether it is truly radical or really the culturally-defined cliche of radicalism. In asking this question we might alight on an interesting essay by Cindy Milstein. Milstein begins by questioning the radicalism of much of the anarchist art she sees at protest rallies. 'Why is anarchist art so often a parody of itself, predictable and uninteresting?' she writes. And why does so much anarchist art seem to 'recreate the aesthetic of destruction' as if 'revelling in the rubble' of what capitalism does to people. Alternatively, she says, we see a carnivalesque approach, exemplified by puppeteering which is so uniform and homogenous it amounts to a kind of 'Wal-Martisation' of resistance art. That which appears to be anarchist art seems, to judge from Milstein's analysis, to have been reified, ceasing to have a vitality rooted in individual aesthetic experiences of the world. It has instead become a style, or rather it has become culture.

As this suggests, even in anarchist circles the notion of a pre-determined definition of radicalism is not absent, and arguably this has always been the case. For example, it appears in Proudhon's discussion of Gustave Courbet's art, where Proudhon argues that art should not be idealist, but morally enlightening. 'The task of art,' Proudhon said, 'is to warn us, to praise us, to teach us, to make us blush by confronting us with the mirror of our own conscience.' Yet as the novelist Émile Zola pointed out, what right had Proudhon to pre-determine the outcome of art in this way, seeming to preach freedom to everyone *except the artist.* 'My art,' wrote Zola, 'is a negation of society, an affirmation of the individual, independent of all rules and all social obligation.' As such it might fulfil the requirements of radical art put forward by Proudhon, but equally it might not.

More recently Patricia Leighten has followed in Proudhon's footsteps by trying to pre-define what constitutes radical anarchist art in her discussion of Juan Gris. In her 1995 essay, 'Réveil anarchiste: Salon Painting, Political Satire, Modernist Art', Leighten contrasts Gris as a maker of political cartoons with Gris as a painter of still lives, saying that one is anarchist the other is not. She writes that by 1909 Gris had, 'self-consciously drained his paintings of political import, avoiding such anarchist subjects as prostitutes [sic]... and neutralising his radical style.'[12] Once again, in this form anarchism here seems to be demanding artists conform to a pre-determined template to define their work as radical. Cartoons of prostitutes are anarchist; paintings of bottles, playing cards and fruit are not.

As you will recall, Zola said, 'My art is a negation of society, an affirmation of the individual.' But there is a much closer relationship between this statement and both Gill and Read's cry of to hell with culture, and my allegory of the bus. To step outside of culture, or step off the bus, is radical because it is to step into the truly unknown, which is inevitably 'the radically different' from the known. In terms of Roland Barthes's hugely influential essay 'The Rhetoric of the Image', it is to abandon the known elements of culture embodied in his definition of connotative and denotive signs and signifiers, and enter into the unknown world of the abyss, *mise en abyme*.

Evidence for this in Zola's rebuke to Proudhon is stark and direct. As artists, Zola claimed, we are not bound by the known laws and strictures of the earth. Instead, 'We are fully in heaven and we are not coming down.' Heaven is a curious word for a consummate realist like Zola to use. To be in heaven is, in Christian terms, to be outside the known world of creation, or one might even say outside known existence. Although at a popular level this is often depicted as the cliché of heaven with its pearly gates or the Garden of Eden, for Christian theologians themselves Heaven is an unknown place, outside the strictures of society and culture. As Eastern Orthodox theologians have called it, heaven is the 'divine darkness'. In that it is the ultimate utopia as it is the ultimate statement of radical difference to the profane light of the known world of culture, society and state institutions.

For bourgeois-marxists an existence outside culture is not conceivable, but as we see, for some anarchists, such as Read, that is the ultimate goal of anarchism, to free the individual from pre-determined culture. In that context radicalism in art is surely not for the anarchist the adoption of pre-determined and ultimately clichéd radical culture, rather it is the escape from culture *per se:* it is the longing of the human soul to get off of the bus.

The Table Top Schools of Art

In some ways an alternative title for this essay, and the talk on which it was originally based, might be, *tolerance isn't all it's cracked up to be.*

Although I like to think of myself as a liberal-minded and tolerant person in most things, when it comes to art education, my previous view that art schools and university art departments should be tolerant and accepting of all that students might want to do in them, has undergone significant change. I am tempted to say I now think art schools and university art departments should be more *intolerant,* but I would only say that with the rider that they are already pretty obdurate places if only people would admit it. Consequently, what might be preferable would be for those art schools and university art departments to simply start acknowledging their biases on their websites and in their prospectuses instead of peddling the lie that they are all things to all people.

I should state that this change of view on my part has not been reached without some regret. I have a longstanding love affair with art schools. It is not only the spaces occupied by art schools that have, for as long as I can remember, seemed to me like gateways to extraordinary other worlds, looking and smelling as mysterious and enticing as any great cathedral or temple, but the people you found in them. Perhaps there were extremes of what the rest of the world calls the artistic temperament, but on the whole art schools were always the most tolerant places on earth for difference, individuality and originality. Not always, but for the most part. So to advocate the abandonment of this art school tolerance is a dramatic shift in my thinking. Yet it comes from an unassailable belief that the things we call art schools today, almost invariably university art departments, are not the beautiful spaces full of beautiful people that characterised the art schools they replaced. University art departments are full of people who think like academics and against academic thought one should always show a deep disdain bordering on intolerance.

Proof of this came to me a few years ago, in 2007, when I was asked to give a talk at the Courtauld Institute of Art in London at a conference organised by Peter Dent, entitled *Sculpture and Touch*. For the most part this was an enjoyable event, except at one of the ubiquitous tea breaks where the talk of the group I stood with turned from the conference to events at the university art department at which one of the other delegates taught. The boast of this delegate was that she had finally got rid of the other members of staff in her department who disagreed with her. Some of them had been there for years, she said, so getting rid of them wasn't easy.

I was shocked by this and left the group in a bad mood. The idea of tolerance and difference in art schools seemed violated, but the cruelty in pushing presumably older members of staff onto the dole and then boasting about it seemed inhuman. Having heard the delegate's conference paper I also knew that had I worked at her university I would probably also be branded one of those who disagreed with her.

In my mind I guess the sheer nastiness of this confirmed my own bad opinion of university art departments. To me the art school had been an anarchistic space, free from the strictures of university learning outcomes and course syllabi, and able to allow students to pursue the open-ended exploration of creativity that is essential to art. In universities those learning outcomes, assessment criteria, learning objectives and course syllabi seemed to be paramount, alongside an obsession with a fetishisation of certificates and documented learning. Art schools seemed vital, universities to suck the joy out of life. No wonder the intolerance of the conference delegate flourished in her university environment, it was an intolerant environment in itself, inimitable to the very creativity it claimed to teach. No doubt, I thought, the intolerant bastard I met at the Courtauld had couched her reasons for the sacking of numerous colleagues and the rewriting of the course programme in ways the intolerant institution would appreciate. At the end of year one, the robot art student will be programmed to do A, B and C, and by the end of year three the robot student will have been programmed to perform functions X, Y and Z. From A to Z in three years. As for the art student who does not want to be a robot, who does not want to move from A to Z in a formulaic and predetermined way, they would presumably be beaten into shape by the academic system of grading or, if too obtuse, asked to leave the institution. The intolerance of the tutors is thus matched by the intolerance of the institution.

The incompatibility of this approach to art education should be obvious, but to spell it out, it is a system that rewards conformity to pre-determined outcomes (those learning outcomes and assessment criteria), whereas the only real justification for the existence of art is its ability to transgress those pre-determined outcomes and reveal to us the unknown. To reveal to us the forms of things unknown, as Herbert Read so memorably called it, quoting Shakespeare. By this criteria there is a good case to argue that the less successful an art student at their university art studies the better an artist they will probably be, although there is an obvious flaw in that theory.

In a liberal frame of mind this might seem to suggest a need to return to the old art school system, outside of the universities, without set syllabi and allowing open-ended processes for the exploration of creativity. The problem with that idea is it is based on a beautiful fallacy, at least on my part, that art schools in olden times really were bastions of tolerance, acceptance and diversity.

My father told the story of going to Leeds College of Art in the 1950s where the college employed a full time member of staff, called Mr Heaps, solely to teach life drawing in a beautiful and specially-built Victorian life drawing room. But Mr Heaps had no students. He sat in the life drawing room, with a model, all day every day, and never saw a single student. The reason for this was the dominant art tutors in the college had such a dislike for the style of realist and classical life drawing Mr Heaps taught they ordered the students to stay away.

A decade later, in the 1960s, almost every art school in England and Ireland saw their own students rise up and literally smash their collections of classical plaster-cast sculptures. As a result, very few art schools in England now have any of these casts, which were once used to teach art students classical drawing, and the last time I saw one in Ireland it was covered in graffiti and being used to decorate a student union bar. Although we might think of this as evidence of spontaneous student revolt, I am told that at Leeds College of Art it was the tutors who incited the students to destroy the casts, and even joined in.

Of course, with the sidelining of Mr Heaps and the smashing of the sculpture casts an old world order was destroyed, but it begs the question, at what point does an act of radicalism become an act of indoctrination? At what point does it become the arrogance of vanguardism?

At my university this kind of indoctrination was explicit. The studio tutors stated very clearly that no student was to paint. Painting was bourgeois, patriarchal and reactionary, and was not permitted in the studios. I have a direct memory of a student almost failing the year for daring to flout this ban. Again, perhaps banning painting was a radical act, but doesn't banning painting or denigrating the classical tradition in art to the point of its literal destruction represent a choking off of the infinite number of possible paths an art student might follow? The result is that not only can a student *not* follow a particular path because of impediments in his or her way, but there is an inevitable implication for the student that by pursuing painting or drawing the work they produce must be irrelevant and backward. In the end this would mean intolerant tutors no longer need to enforce their bans as the indoctrination would make this intolerance part of the students' own psychological make up.

It is tempting to despair at this state of affairs. It suggests that even without institutional bias closing down the necessary principle of art that requires artists and art students to engage in open-ended artistic enquiry, art students will still face individual bias from tutors whose preference for a particular kind of artistic practice will be accompanied by a similar closing-off of the possibility of other kinds of artistic practice. Is that what motivated Herbert Read to tell the painter Victor Willing in an interview in 1960 that the best thing that could happen to promote a world of truly vital art would be to close down the art schools? The art schools Read suggested, long before they had university-type academic systems imposed on them, were bad for art because they taught cliches of art not the capacity to make art itself. It is the closing down of the infinite number of possible directions by whatever means that results in pre-determined cliches. Indeed, almost thirty years earlier Read saw the same problem of intolerance and partisanship closing down the possibilities of art in the wider art world, and argued instead that we should strive for an anarchist society in which, 'each type of artist could express himself in the manner which he found most apt. Constructivists and superrealists, realists and expressionists, could live and work side by side in perfect amity.' As Read suggested here, the failure to have a world like this at the moment should not be the source of despair. 'I do not suggest that such a community of individuals is too idealistic to contemplate,' he said. 'It is the ideal towards which we should aim.'[13]

The questions are what would a community like this be like and how can it be achieved?

Following my sense of shock at being a silent witness to the conversation at the Courtauld conference tea break, and my own experiences in university art departments as both a student and tutor, my inclination is to suggest that perhaps it is better to approach this problem from a different angle. Rather than saying rather feyly, wouldn't it be nice if everyone could just get on and be nice to each other – living and working side by side in perfect amity, dare I say – what if we instead rethink our admiration for tolerance, acceptance and pluralism in art schools to ask whether it is an over-rated concept. Perhaps the model I knew as a student, for all its intolerance of particular practises, was in some respects a good model because at least I knew where I stood in relation to it.

In my own case, my nascent interest in Herbert Read and anarchist ideas on art and culture were not widely tolerated in the explicitly pro-marxist art department in which I studied, and this led me to look elsewhere for the encouragement I needed to pursue my interests. Had I simply been accepted and tolerated within the department, no doubt some things would have been easier, but two other things would have happened. First I would have found myself being taught about Herbert Read and anarchism by people with no interest in (and a hidden disdain for) those topics. From a pedagogical point of view that does not seem healthy or desirable. And secondly, those tutors themselves would be forced to fein an interest in (and undertake the teaching of) subjects they personally disliked. Perhaps we might argue that is sometimes the job of the teacher, but as a student I am not sure I would have wanted to be taught by someone with a half-cocked interest in what I thought was important. I would have wanted sympathetic support, and luckily, outside the mainstream tutors of my university department I was able to find that support.

What this suggests to me is there needs to be an ability for students to bypass the dominant institutional frameworks for art education, and that this will create the opportunity for them to study art with the freedom of their own inclinations. At the same time it would not shackle every art tutor to the requirement to teach aspects of art in which they do not have absolute faith. In this what we need is to completely rethink what we mean by an art school, taking it away from the closed structures of the academic system and the privileged biases of a small number of tutors who are dominant in that system.

In my thinking the model for this stems from something the artist Peter de Francia once said about the Cyprus College of Art. Founded in 1969 by my father, Stass Paraskos, the Cyprus College of Art did not resemble other art schools in either shape or form. By this I mean it did not look like what my father used to call a 'respectable' art school. Rather it was collection of ramshackle buildings, hand-built from ply-board and timber by the first artists and art students to use the place. These structures were the studios and they were surrounded by an overgrown garden of citrus and mulberry trees. The place 'lacked' an office, and had no library or any form of computer facility. In all of that it was not a respectable art school, and the Ministry of Education in Cyprus often threatened to close it down because of this. But under my father it also did not act like a respectable art school because it embodied his absolute disdain for course documents, pre-determined learning outcomes and formal qualifications. Again, this caused serious tensions with the Ministry of Education, which objected to the Cyprus College of Art because it refused to conform to the cliche as to what constituted an art school. It was instead so fully orientated around my father, and the small group of artist friends he worked with, that if a student went there it was because they also wanted to work with them.

I do stress that did not mean the art students who went to the Cyprus College of Art necessarily wanted to make work that looked like that of my father or the other artists at the College, rather that the environment that had been created there was one in which they wanted to orientate their own visual practice.

Focusing on this de Francia suggested that the Cyprus College of Art proved that an art school does not need to be called a university, or have fancy studios, or high tech equipment, or learning outcomes and syllabi. To create an art school you simply need to get four artists together under a tree. As soon as they start talking you have an art school.

This is an extraordinary idea that has great resonance at this particular moment in time when so many people around the world seem dissatisfied with institutions of formal art education. It suggests we can redefine what an art school really is, taking it out of the university sector completely, but also allowing artists the right to hold their preferences for and against different art forms. To paraphrase Herbert Read, constructivists and superrealists, realists and expressionists, can live and work side by side in perfect amity without necessarily agreeing with each other. If your orientation as an art student is more toward 'constructivism' than 'superrealism' (or rather their latter day equivalents) then it make sense not to try to study constructivism in an art school that is openly geared towards superrealism. Instead the student would be better advised studying at an art school of constructivists. However, for this to work, we would need an almost infinite number of art schools, each geared towards a different approach. The only way for this situation to exist would be for us to forget about an art school being a place where students study to get diplomas and degrees and instead see it as a gathering of like-minded artists, meeting, working and organising together, and sharing ideas. This would be to accept that each particular art school might be 'intolerant' of the preferences of another art school, but that would not matter because of the infinite plurality of the situation. In a sense every artist would become an art school, free to assemble in whatever combination they wanted with any other artist.

The point here is to get away from the cliched notion of an educational institution, so that we might well say that if four artists gather together under a tree that is an art school. Similarly four artists around a kitchen table. Or four artists in the café, or a bar, or an Indian Restaurant.

By redefining the art school in this way we also redefine what it means to be a student in an art school, turning the art school into a more co-operative environment in which the student and tutor work together not for meaningless pieces of paper that certify someone is an artist, but in a search for creative experiences. That would in itself remove the palpable sense of despair that we can see crippling the creative spirit in university art departments today as both art students and art tutors are faced with inescapably coercive systems.

A system of table-top schools of art would be the means to find new ways of meeting as artists, art educators and art students, of forging alliances, connections and even friendships, bringing back the sense of joy that should be inherent in the pursuit of art. If we abandon the idea that art schools are big institutions with libraries, and well-appointed studios, and computer rooms, we end up with the art school as simply any place where artists meet and discuss art. The art school becomes a table top school of art, one in the kitchen or living room of every artist's home, in which the realist painter doesn't have to like the work of the conceptualist installation artist, and the video artist does not have to like the idea of bronze casting, but where they each simply get on with their own thing.

I like the unpredictable grass roots aspect of hundreds, and perhaps thousands, of impromptu art schools springing up and replacing the faux tolerance of institutional university art departments. But I also believe the responsive and fluid nature of this approach will be stronger and more connected to the flow of life than any grand cultural scheme for art education imposed from above.

An Anarchist
in Heaven and Hell

Reverbstorm is a book by David Britton and John Coulthart, which I first reviewed, in what a number of people have considered the unlikely setting of *The Spectator* magazine,[14] back in March 2013.[15] Unlikely or not, it was the then book editor of *The Spectator,* Mark Amory, who suggested I review the book, reiterating the fact that, whatever the political views of that magazine, when it came to literature it was always a more open and diverse publication than many of its more liberal-left rivals – at least when Mark was selecting the books for review.

This relative openness was particularly necessary in relation to *Reverbstorm,* I suspect, as it was a book published by the Savoy Press in Manchester, a publishing house that frequently found itself as reviled as much by the left for its lack of political correctness as by the right for attacking the shibboleths of authority. As I said in my original review, in this I think the Savoy Press embodies a longstanding tradition of non-conformist thinking in English cultural life that is essentially anarchistic, even if not explicitly anarchist.

Although *Reverbstorm* is a book, it is a

graphic novel. This created some difficulties for me as I do not claim to be knowledgeable on that genre, and any possible referencing of *Reverbstorm* to the graphic novel or comic book tradition would surely have passed me by. Added to this, despite my childhood love of Asterix at one extreme and the comic books in the *Tales from the Crypt* series, bought by my brother when we were children, from a somewhat dubious shop in Chapeltown Road in Leeds, on visits to my grandmother, I could not claim to have the experience behind me of reading visual narratives like this. Indeed, the supreme irony in Mark giving me a graphic novel to read was that in terms of art I have a longstanding history of arguing that too much emphasis is given in our society to the meaning or narrative of visual art, rather than its inherent visual qualities.

My solution to the problems these issues threw up was simple. I treated the book as a work of visual art, rather than a novel, an approach that undoubtedly leaves the way open for other interpretations to come along and fill in the gaps I have left (or missed). But I make no apologies for approaching *Reverbstorm* in this way as it was the only way that was true to myself.

Reverbstorm is part of the long-running Lord Horror series, and is set in a nightmarish dreamscape where a fantasy 1930s New York is fused with the death camps at Auschwitz. Although presented in a single volume, the book began life in 1994 as an adult comic, published in the tradition of Dickens as a piece-work. It is tempting to say that is where the comparison with nineteenth-century literature ends, but the mire of Dickens's world, where stories of callous modernity and human degradation go hand in hand, runs throughout *Reverbstorm*.

Unlike Dickens, however, there is a question whether there is a story in *Reverbstorm* at all. There is the central motif of the psychopath, Lord Horror, a pun on the British wartime traitor Lord Haw-Haw, who stalks the streets repeatedly slashing people, mainly Jews, with a cut-throat razor. Like Haw-Haw, Horror has his own radio show, to which we cut in the sequence of images periodically, but beyond a Joycean tour around the fantasy city of Torenburgen it is difficult to outline a clear narrative thread.

The images of evisceration in the drawings are explicit, as is the sex and language, but as I tried to explain in my review, the idea *Reverbstorm* should be dismissed as a kind of graphic novel porn, glorifying the Third Reich and degrading humanity, is to miss an essential point. The reason it was possible for me to review *Reverbstorm* as a work of art was simply that it is a work of art, and on that basis it is simply wrong to apply the standards or behaviour, and more particularly the morality of everyday life, to it. Like all art, *Reverbstorm* is derived from aspects of life, but art is not life. Art is a special (and in an earlier age we might have said scared) space that exists outside life, and from that undeniably privileged position it allows humanity to posit new ways of living, formulate alternative conceptions of reality and, of course, also face up to genuine horror. Noel Carroll made this point rather nicely when he wrote: 'Art-horror is the price we are willing to pay for the revelation of that which is impossible and unknown, of that which violates our conceptual schema.'[16]

If we think of one of the most successful patrons of art ever to exist in human history, the Christian Church, this role of art has been absolutely understood. While a Noddy reading of art history might want to present Christian art as merely a kind of tool for indoctrination, the fact is Christian art has long recognised that the world of art and the world of life are two distinct things, and this suggests a far more complex understanding of the necessity of art. Nowhere is this more apparent than in the traditions of the eastern Orthodox Church where the painted icon is conceptualised as a 'celestial window', allowing the viewer to gaze into another world.[17]

For the Orthodox Church that other world is a kind of heaven, although we need to be careful in what we mean by words like heaven and its synonym, paradise. Both heaven and paradise are polluted terms in modern language, tending to mean something pleasant, like a holiday paradise or the joy of heaven on earth. For Orthodox theologians, at least, heaven has never been so mundane. For Vladimir Lossky what defines God as God is his unknowability to non-gods. In other words God is unknowable to human beings. From that it follows that God must be radically different from anything that a human might know, and from that it is reasonable to assume in turn that God resides in a space that is unknowable to non-gods. God must reside in a kind of divine darkness, always beyond the gaze of human eyes.[18] In this conception of divine space, heaven or paradise is clearly not like the best thing on earth only better. It is the radical other to the world in which we live.[19]

So what do we see when we look through the celestial window of a Greek Orthodox icon painting and gain a glimpse of heaven, what are the images we are shown? Occasionally we might well see a paradisiacal garden, but as likely we will see Christ being forever crucified, St Gideon being dismembered alive, St Stephen being stoned to death, or St Ignatius of Antioch being torn apart by lions. The Orthodox method of viewing heaven through art reveals it to be a space where actions seem as explicit and violent as anything we might to object to on moral grounds in *Reverbstorm*.

As one of the foundation points of Western art, this aspect of the Byzantine Greek Orthodox tradition continued into mainstream Western art, so that there too artists have not necessarily shown us images of pleasure. Rather, in the 'sacred' space beyond the picture plane, we see Titian's *Flaying of Marsyas*, Artemisia Gentileschi's *Judith Beheading Holofernes* and David's *Death of Marat*. We see Francis Bacon painting the suicide of his lover George Dyer. The point about examples such as these is that the painted space, the space I have called, 'beyond the picture plane', is outside of our reality, and not a straightforward reflection of our reality. They operate more like worlds through a looking glass, each with its own distinct moral, narrative and spatial code, and not as mirrors held up to our world. It is in this context that *Reverbstorm* has to be judged, not as a bad book because we do not like Nazi psychopaths shown in such an exuberant and unrepentant fashion, but as the vision of another reality in which Nazi psychopaths exist in an exuberant and unrepentant fashion. To look at art has to be to accept that art is another reality, and they do things differently there.

The sense of alternative realities can seem very alien to anarchist thinking, which is often predicated on a material realist basis, stressing the existence of only one world, the world in which we live, and rejecting all metaphysical speculation. The Christian promise of a pleasant heaven when we die, having lived a good life, is often seen as a fallacy designed specifically to enforce compliance with a moral code that supports a particular set of social relationships. And yet few forms of radical political ideology have been as supportive of art, or as supported by artists, as anarchism.[20] In that relationship, art has not had to abandon the concept of imaginative transcendence, and from the earliest days of anarchism this was accepted as one of the key strengths of art. A key precursor to modern anarchism, Charles Fourier, even adopted methods derived from art, and specifically the theology of religious art, to imagine what a post-revolutionary anarchistic world would be like.

Writing in the early years of the nineteenth century, Fourier suggested that after a revolution not only would social, economic and political relationships change, but the nature of reality would be different, just as the nature of reality is different in Christian art and eschatology. For Fourier in a post-revolutionary utopia lions and sharks would cease to be dangerous meat-eating animals and turn instead into vegetarian anti-lions and anti-sharks. Similarly the salty sea that is poisonous to drink would be magically transformed into harmless lemonade. Whether Fourier believed these things would happen literally has been hotly debated from the outset, but the real point about Fourier's utopia is that he makes the case that any revolution, if it is to deserve the name of revolution, must necessarily result in a situation revolutionarily different to the situation now. It is not hard to map this view onto the eastern Orthodox Christian conception of God and heaven, where the difference between our world and the posited other world must also necessarily be profound.

A more direct connection between this way of thinking and anarchism was made by Herbert Read, who even adopted the language of eastern Orthodox Christianity in proposing that art operates as the mediator between the known world we inhabit and the unknown world to which we seek access, by acting as the intermediary between the two. In Orthodox theology this mediating role is called hypostasis, and through it Read is suggesting that like the

Orthodox Christian icon, all art here acts as a kind of celestial window between the known and the unknown. As Read described it, art is an 'intermediary between the world of natural phenomena and the world of spiritual presences.'[21]

It is not unreasonable to assume that Read's basic reasoning on this came directly from a number of Russian avant-garde artists he knew in the 1930s, particularly Kandinsky, brought up in the eastern Orthodox Christian tradition.

The language of spiritualism used by Read might lead us to dismiss his theory from a materialist perspective, but the notion of some kind of transcendence through art is not unique to him in anarchist writings. Writing on Kika Thorne sculpture *Octave* (2009), Allan Antliff claimed:

> If, while viewing the work, you gaze into *Octave's* suspended mirror (which casts an array of reflections and shadows traversing the gallery wall and flooring), you will discover the multi- coloured cords that give Octave sculptural form expand outward, creating a dizzying 'parallel world' delimited by pristine geometrics reminiscent of anarchist sculptor Naum Gabo's crystalline representations of organic structures

in nature. Octave demonstrates abstract art's ability to move beyond self-referential concerns, infusing sensate experience with aesthetic qualities that approach the sublime.[22]

What I think is important here in relation to *Reverbstorm* is that transcendence in this context is not necessarily a question of mystical otherness, although it is almost invariably a question of mysterious otherness – the sublime of which Allan Antliff writes. Primarily it is a question of otherness itself, the essential difference between our reality and the alternative realities of works of art such as *Reverbstorm*. If that alternative reality was to function like our reality, in its moral codes and questions of taste, it would negate its own essential otherness, as much as turning God into an old man with a beard negates the divinity of God by making him all too human. It is the very otherness of art that allows it to posit alternative ways of being in the first place, both good and bad, establishing an alternative reality in which the lion can become a gentle vegetarian, as suggested by Fourier, or act as the tool to martyr a Christian saint. In the context of art the question of moral 'goodness' or 'badness' can never really matter, only the question of radical 'otherness'. And it is that otherness to our reality that sets up the fundamental connection between art and anarchism, with each seeking to strip away the inherent (and for our society bourgeois) realism of our world to reveal a very different alternative.

That all sounds very nice, and of course any artist might claim they show us other worlds and other ways of being. Others might complain that this is all very well in theory, but what does in mean in practise? I have spent most of my working life with art students in practical art schools and I believe the answer to that question is simpler than it might at first appear. To be faced with a blank canvas on a wall or an easel is to be faced with a choice of infinite possibilities. On that canvas the artist or art student might reveal to us anything. The question is, will they reveal what is already known, repeating familiar subjects, stories, methods of working and organising space, ways of applying paint and so on, or will they seek to break out of those known and cliched tropes and discover something unknown. It is the discovery of the unknown, the unexpected phrase of paint, or colour, or form, or space, that turns the canvas from a mirror reflecting that which is already known, to a portal into the unknown. And in this, the primary tool in the tool box of the art studio is always the artists' heartfelt intentions. As with every other anarchist, whether they choose to call themselves by that name or not, to be satisfied with reflecting the cliched, the familiar and the known is to restrict oneself to the cliched, the familiar and the known. To be dissatisfied with those easy answers, on the other hand, and to seek out with a sense of hope and ambition the spaces of art and society that are unexpected, unrevealed and unknown, is to at least hold out the possibility of finding them.

The Canvas
as Commune

Once upon a time all art was a collaborative process. No painting by Michelangelo, or Rubens, or Rembrandt was ever the sole product of the artists who bore those names. They were each helped by studio assistants, many of whom had great skill and talent.

Assistants did more than simply grind the paint and hold the brushes. Often they helped form some of the great works of western art, including such wonders as the Sistine Chapel ceiling. As Jerry Brotton states in his book *The Renaissance Bazaar,* works like the Sistine Chapel ceiling were group efforts rather than the creation of one individual man.[23]

In modern times too artworks we think of as being by one artist were in fact made by a group of people. August Rodin used many studio assistants, including Antoine Bourdelle, Camille Claudel and Francois Pompon. The same is true of Henry Moore, despite his stated belief in the importance of sculptors carving their own work. In fact Moore's assistants included some of the most well-regarded sculptors of the twentieth century, including Reg Butler, Anthony Caro and Phillip King. They were not his students, they were his assistants, and each played a part in the creation of Moore's artworks.

In the collaboration between Stephan Metaxas, Stass Paraskos and Stelios Votsis we saw a similar phenomenon. The paintings they made together were a group effort, albeit a small group of three. Yet there was a crucial difference between their way of working and that of the Old or Modern Masters. In the case of Michelangelo, Rodin and Moore, the studio assistants were required to suppress their own individuality in the making of art and be guided by their master. The role of the master was to act almost like the director of a play or the conductor of an orchestra, and the studio assistants were required to do exactly what he said. The master then gave his name to the artwork that was produced. However, Metaxas and Paraskos were not the 'studio assistants' of Votsis, and Votsis was not the 'studio assistant' of either Metaxas or Paraskos. Their group was egalitarian and each contributed to the making of their collaborative paintings in equal measure.

Of course other artists collaborate in producing their work. Not long ago the Cyprus College of Art was fortunate in having the British sculptors Eve Bennett and Chris Rutter as artists-in-residence, and it was possible to see at first hand in the extraordinary yellow tower sculpture they produced how two people would combine to produce a single work of art, not in a master-servant relationship, but as equal parters. Of course, this can also be seen in the working method of Gilbert and George, and the example of the English-Cypriots Jake and Dinos Chapman. In each case there is no known sense of one of the partners dominating the other – although we cannot know what really happens in the privacy of their studios, behind closed doors. Instead there is a sense of each side being engaged in a partnership of equals.

In this there is a marked difference to the use of studio assistants by historical artists, but also by other contemporaries, such as Anthony Gormley and Damien Hirst, where the master-servant relationship still appears to be practised. But there is also a marked difference between the approach of Rutter and Bennett, the Chapman Brothers and Gilbert and George on one side, and the approach of Metaxas, Paraskos and Votsis on the other. With Rutter and Bennett you could not say which part of their work was made by Rutter and which by Bennett, just as there is no way of telling which idea in the work of the Chapmans came from Jake and which from Dinos. But that was not the case with the collaborative paintings of Metaxas, Paraskos and Votsis. In them there was no attempt made to merge their separate ways of working into a single style. Metaxas remained Metaxas, Paraskos remained Paraskos and Votsis remained Votsis, and you could point out their individual contributions to each painting very easily. In essence they each remained individuals within what was the shared space of the painted canvas.

Each of the three artists knew that such a working method was very dangerous. Although a painting can tell a story, or symbolise an emotional state, or comment on social and political life, the primary purpose of all painting is to define or open up a believable sense of space. This has always been the primary function of painting, its reason for existence. Through the creation of a space conceptually outside the space we inhabit in our reality an arena is opened up in which stories, or emotions, or ideological beliefs can be imagined and explored. Of course the space that an artist opens up on a canvas is not necessarily like the space we occupy in our everyday lives. In fact it can be a very different type of space, as in an abstract painting or a church icon. Indeed, it is that difference to our own reality that makes the painted space such a potent and radical tool for revolutionary thought, establishing another reality outside our reality in which other forms of life can be imagined and brought into being.

Yet, if that imagined space is not going to descend into meaningless fantasy it must be, in some sense, believable to allow the viewer to be convinced by it. The viewer has to be persuaded to allow what is called the 'suspension of disbelief. Fail to open up a believable space and you could have the world's greatest story, or emotional epiphany, or political manifesto to convey, but no one will believe it because the space in which it is set is unbelievable. It would remain a fantasy.

As I have said, this is not an argument for space that is realist or which emulates space in our world. Abstract space in abstract art is just as likely to be believable as realist space in realist art. In either case what is necessary to create believable space in a painting is aesthetic coherency. This means that all the elements in a painting must be related to each other through a coherent aesthetic system, which is sometimes called rhythm.

To understand this one can think about the way the universe in which we live is governed by the series of laws we call the laws of physics. These laws encompass many different things, but together they form the coherent framework in which we live. We might call this framework the 'rhythm of physics'. In painting, however, the artist can discard the rhythm of physics and establish her own rhythm, whether it is realist, figurative, abstracted or wholly abstract. Tradition in art dictates that once that rhythm is established all the elements of the picture must relate to it, and as long as this happens the painting will be coherent and believable no matter what it shows or how it shows it.

The danger with the collaborative working method of Metaxas, Paraskos and Votsis was that Metaxas could work to one rhythm, Paraskos to another and Votsis to another still. To avoid this other artists have either imposed the single authoritarian rhythm of the master on all those working beneath him, as in the case of Anthony Gormley or Damien Hirst, or they have negotiated a single rhythm through co-operation, as with Rutter and Bennett or Gilbert and George. But Metaxas, Paraskos and Votsis chose a different path by simply maintaining their own aesthetic styles whilst sharing the single space of the canvas. In doing so they risked placing onto that canvas a clashing set of rhythms that might fail to cohere into a single space, and in that failure to cohere, not manage to persuade their viewers to suspend his or her sense of disbelief.

Given the risk of failure in this method it is not surprising few artists, if any, have tried anything like it before. Unsurprising too is that Metaxas, Paraskos and Votsis described their collaboration as an experiment, and as in scientific experiments they acknowledged the outcome is not always successful.

With this in mind there is no doubt some of their early collaborative works did not cohere and did not create a believable pictorial universe. Those painting and drawings were discarded along the way, but out of these early attempts there slowly emerged a series of artworks in which a very remarkable thing happened. Three artists with very different working methods and styles began producing paintings that did cohere, and did so with an increasing level of sophistication. In their early works the Metaxas parts the paintings tended to be very separate from the Paraskos parts of the paintings, which tended in turn to be very separate from the Votsis parts of the paintings, causing some of them to appear almost like three paintings on one canvas. As they continued to work, however, the lines, colours, forms and narratives that were started by one artist were picked up by the others, who would then develop them further before handing them back. This process of alternation could be repeated several times, making the whole process organic and evolutionary. In a very real way, this method of working was less like traditional painting than the way a group of jazz musicians will each play a series of individual solos within a single set, often picking up on what has been played before, but moving it into a new direction.

Like jazz, such co-operation was inherently democratic and undermined the autocracy of the single point of view. It toppled a dictatorship. That dictator was the idea of an artist who forced his views on to his studio assistants, and forced his views on to the canvas, and forced his views on to the spectator. He was a tyrant, a caliph and a tsar, and we can only wonder at how so much beauty could come from so much despotism. In their work, Metaxas, Paraskos and Votsis did something wholly different and extraordinary. It was something so shocking it offended six-hundred years of artistic tradition. In their work they not only opened up space, but they dared to share that space and leave it open to dialogues that often evolved in surprising and unexpected ways. In place of a dictatorship, this revolution turned the painted space into an anarchist commune in which two, or three, or perhaps even an infinite number of artists could negotiate the rhythms of space, or the primary laws of a painting's existence, each in their own individual way.

1 Quoted in Herbert Read, *To Hell with Culture* (London: Routledge, 1963, 2002 reissue) 10

2 Jennifer Uglow and Maggy Hendry, *The Northeastern Dictionary of Women's Biography* (Boston: Northeastern University Press; 3rd edition 1999) 451

3 Victor Willing, 'Interview with Herbert Read', in *Studio International*, September 1960,136f

4 John Molyneux, Review of *Rembrandt's Eyes* by Simon Schama, <http://johnmolyneux.blogspot.co.uk/2006/08/review-of-rembrandts-eyes html> accessed 23 August 2012

5 John Farquhar McLay, *Anarchism and Art* (Glasgow: Autonomy Press, 1982) 3. This booklet was the text of a speech originally given to Glasgow University Libertarian Association on 24 February 1982

6 Taken from the University of St Andrews website page of Professor Brendan Cassidy, Head of Art History. <http://www-ah.st-andrews.ac.uk/staff/brendan.html> accessed 23 August 2012

7 Paul Mattick, *Art in Its Time* (London: Routledge, 2003) 180-1

8 Louise Jury, 'Wallinger: Why I had to win the Turner' in *The London Evening Standard*, 4 December 2007

9 Sinead Murphy, *The Art Kettle* (London: Zero Books, 2012) 2-6

10 See Carey Jewitt and Rumiko Oyama, 'Visual Meaning: A Social Semiotic Approach' in Carey Jewitt and Theo Van Leeuwen, *A Handbook of Visual Analysis* (London: Sage Publications, 2001)

11 John Farquhar McLay, *Anarchism and Art* (Glasgow: Autonomy Press, 1982) p.10.

12 Patricia Leighten, '*Réveil anarchiste*: Salon Painting, Political Satire, Modernist Art', in Josh MacPhee and Erik Reuland (eds.), *Realizing the Impossible: Art Against Authority* (Oakland: AK Press, 2007) 39

13 Herbert Read, *The Politics of the Unpolitical* (London: Routledge, 1943) 116-7

14 Benjamin Noys, 'Full Spectrum Offence: Savoy's Neo-Weird', conference paper delivered at 'The Weird: Fugitive Fictions/Hybrid Genres', at the Institute of English Studies, University of London, 8 November 2013, online version <http://leniency.blogspot.co.uk/2013/11/full-spectrum-offence-savoys-neo-weird.html>accessed 19 September 2015.

15 Review of *Lord Horror: Reverbstorm,* by David Britton and John Coulthart, in *The Spectator,* 9 March 2013

16 Noel Carroll, *The Philosophy of Horror or Paradoxes of the Heart* (New York: Routledge, 1990) 186

17 Ernst Benz, *The Eastern Orthodox Church* (New Brunswick Aldine Transaction, 1957: 2009 reprint) 6

18 Vladimir Lossky, *The Mystical Theology of the Eastern Orthodox Church* (London: James Clarke and Co., 1957) p.23f

19 See Jean-Luc Marion, *God Without Being,* trans. Thomas A. Carlson (Chicago: University of Chicago Press, 1991) 16

20 Donald Drew Egbert, *Social Radicalism and the Arts* (New York: Alfred J. Knopf, 1970) 714f

21 Herbert Read, *Art and Society* (London: William Heinemann, 1937) 80-1

22 Alan Antliff, 'Open Form and the Abstract Imperative: Herbert Read and Contemporary Anarchist Art' in Michael Paraskos (ed.), *Re-Reading Read: New Views on Herbert Read* (London: Freedom Press, 2007) 43

23 Jerry Brotton, *The Renaissance Bazaar* (Oxford: Oxford University Press, 2003)